The Indians
of California

The Center is Supported by Grants from
The National Endowment for the Humanities
The Ford Foundation
The W. Clement and Jessie V. Stone Foundation
The Woods Charitable Fund, Inc.

The Indians of California

A Critical Bibliography

ROBERT F. HEIZER

Published for the Newberry Library

Indiana University Press

BLOOMINGTON

Published in Canada by Fitzhenry & Whiteside Limited, Don Mills Ontario

Manufactured in the United States of America

Library of Congress Cataloging in Publication Data
Heizer, Robert Fleming, 1915-
    Indians of California.
  e Newberry Library Center for the History of
    American Indian bibliographical series)
  Indians of North America—California—Bibliog-
  hy. I. Title. II. Series: Newberry Library,
  cago. Center for the History of the American
  ian. The Newberry Library Center for the His-
  y of the American Indian bibliographical series.
  :09.2.U52C23 1976 [E78.C15] 016.97'0004'97
  -12372
  N 0-253-33001-7   2 3 4 5 6 7 8 83 82

The Editors to the Reader

A massive literature exists for the history and culture of American Indians, but the quality of that literature is very uneven. At its best it compares well with the finest scholarship and most interesting reading to be found anywhere. At its worst it may take the form of malicious fabrication. Sometimes, well-intentioned writers give false impressions of reality either because of their own limitations of mind or because they lack adequate information. The consequence is a kind of chaos through which advanced scholars as well as new students must warily pick their way. It is, after all, a history of hundreds, if not thousands, of human communities spread over an entire continent and enduring through millenia of pre-Columbian years as well as the five centuries that Europeans have documented since 1492. That is not a small amount of history.

Often, however, historians have been so concerned with the affairs of European colonies or the United States that they have almost omitted Indians from their own history. "Frontier history" and the "history of Indian–White relations" frequently focus upon the intentions and desires of Euramericans, treating Native Americans as though they were merely natural parts of the landscape, like forests, or mountains, or wild animals — obstacles to "progress" or "civilization." One of the major purposes of the Newberry Library's Center for the History of the American Indian is to modify that narrow conception; to put Indians properly back into the central role in their own history and into the history of the United States of America as well — as participants in, rather than obstacles to, the creation of American society and culture.

The series of bibliographies, of which this book is one part, is intended as a guide to reliable sources and studies in particular fields of the general literature. Some of these are devoted to culture areas; others treat selected individual tribes; and a third group will speak to significant contemporary and historical issues.

It is hard, however, to put the present work by Professor Heizer into a neatly bounded category, for it embraces readings in all three fields. Here are studies of the Indians of California as a whole as well as of individual tribes; and their history is reviewed from aboriginal times to the present day. It is the guidance of a master scholar through a mountainous labyrinth of literature. What he describes will come as a special surprise to readers who have adopted simplistic (but all too common) conceptions of the march of "civilization" from the Atlantic to the Pacific. They will find here much food for thought in the varied effects of Spanish, Mexican, and United States expansion against tribes who were also varied in their aboriginal cultures.

This work is designed in a format, uniform throughout the entire series, to be useful to both beginning students and advanced scholars. It has two main parts: the essay (conveniently organized by subheadings) and an alphabetical list of all works cited. All citations in the essay are directly keyed, by means of bracketed numbers, to the more complete information in the list. In addition, the series incorporates several information-at-a-glance features. Preceding the list will be found two sets of recommended titles. One of these is a list of five items for the beginner; the second, a group of volumes that constitute a basic library collection in the field. Finally, asterisks within the alphabetical list denote works suitable for secondary school students. This apparatus has been built-in because the bibliographical essay, in a form familiar to scholars, will probably prove fairly hard going for beginners who may wish to put it aside until they have gained sufficient background from introductory materials. Such students should come back to the essay eventually, however, because it surveys a vast sweep of information about a great variety of persons, places, communities, and events.

There is variety also in the kinds of sources because these critical bibliographies support the study of ethnohistory. Unlike older, more narrow disciplines, ethnohistory embraces the entire culture of a people; it demands contributions from a wide range of source materials. Not the least of these in the history of American Indians are their own music, crafts, linguistics, and oral traditions. Whenever possible, the authors have included such sources as well as those associated with politics, economics, geography, and so on.

In the last analysis this work, like all other bibliographical devices, is a tool. Each author is an expert who knows the literature and advises what source is most helpful for which purpose, but students must use this help according to their individual purposes and capacities. Many ways suggest themselves. The decision is the reader's own.

Introduction

Everything ever written, or to be written, about the Indians of California is in some way a record of the history of these people. A full bibliography of California Indian history, therefore, would run to a volume of substantial size. Offered here is a guide to some works of basic importance for introducing the reader to the subject. Titles selected are from a list about four times as large which has recently appeared in print.*

When California Indian history begins we do not yet know. Evidence from archaeology shows that the land was occupied as early as about 11,000 years ago. There have been numerous claims that occupance can be pushed back to 25,000 or even 100,000 years ago, but there are persuasive reasons for not accepting these propositions. In the course of time new archaeological finds will settle the question of how long ago California was first occupied.

Juan Rodriguez Cabrillo discovered California in 1542. It was visited subsequently by Sir Francis Drake in 1579 and Sebastian Vizcaino in 1602. The Indian population at this time has been set at about 300,000 by Sherburne F. Cook in *The Population of the California Indians, 1769–1970* [48], the most intensive demographic survey of the subject ever written. Not until 1769 did actual

*Robert F. Heizer, Karen M. Nissen, and Edward D. Castillo. 1975. *California Indian History; A Classified and Annotated Guide to Source Materials.* Ballena Press Publications in Archaeology, Ethnology and History:4, ed. Robert F. Heizer. Ramona, Calif.:Ballena Press.

settlement by Europeans occur here, the reason being the establishment of a series of missions administered by the Franciscan order extending from San Diego in the south to Sonoma in the north. The Native Californian victims of this religious enterprise learned nothing useful to them. It is not wrong to characterize the mission period (1769–1834) as an unmitigted disaster for the coastal tribes. In this span of sixty-five years, 54,000 persons were converted. In the missions there were 29,000 recorded births and 62,000 deaths. Diseases introduced by the Spanish were communicated to unconverted "gentiles" or "heathens" (as the missionaries called them) in the interior with consequent heavy death tolls as a result. By the end of the mission period, there were about 100,000 surviving Native Californians. After the Mexican revolution (1821) and secularization of the missions (1834), there was a period of relative calm — one rudely shattered by the seizure of California in 1846 by United States naval and military forces (an early action of the Mexican War). Then followed the Gold Rush, initiated by the discovery of this metal at Sutter's sawmill at Coloma on 24 January 1848. The horde of gold miners descended on the Sierra Nevada, an area hitherto untouched by the Spaniards or Mexicans. The American invasion reduced the surviving native population, numbering about 100,000 in 1848, to about 50,000 to 30,000 (calculations differ on this figure). Further decrease, a result of neglect as well as the continuance of pervasive processes set in motion during earlier decades, brought the native population to about 20,000 in 1910, according to Kroeber's calculation [130]. It has gradually increased to number (together with representatives of immigrant tribal groups) about 90,000 in 1975.

The first serious and systematic ethnography in California was carried out by Stephen Powers, a journalist of great perceptiveness, whose collected magazine articles appeared in 1877 under the title *Tribes of California* [157]. In 1901, with the establishment of the Department of Anthropology at the University of California under the direction of F. W. Putnam and Alfred L. Kroeber, there began an intensive program of recording tribal ethnographies, languages, and mythology. This effort continued up to the beginning of World War II. Scores of tribes were studied and reported on in scientific articles and monographs. These were all cast in the "ethnographic present" — a term which implied by the use of the present tense that the unaltered and pristine native culture was being described. In some, though rare cases, this may have been true, but when informants born in 1870 or 1880 or 1900 or 1920 were being interviewed, there can be no doubt whatsoever that they were reporting culture facts very much altered during the preceding one hundred to one hundred fifty years of Spanish–Mexican–American occupation. There is little question, though it may be impossible to prove, that the aboriginal tribal distribution (as represented to portray the situation in 1770 and prepared on the basis of records made by several score of ethnographers) is in part a historic artifact. Tribes became extinct without even their names being recorded, their former presence almost beyond recollection. Shifts of territory due to the vacating of lands through demographic decline most certainly occurred. The unravelling and reweaving of this historical fabric stands today as the great opportunity for students of Native American history.

The Study of Indian Civilization

No single work adequately covers the history of Native Californians since their discovery four hundred years ago or from the time of initial European settlement slightly over two hundred years ago. The California historian Hubert Howe Bancroft managed to include a good deal of information on this subject in his encyclopedic seven-volume *History of California* [9], but Bancroft was really writing the Caucasian history of the state and his Indian affairs are cast in this perspective. Bancroft's bias was pointed out by Zephyrin Engelhardt, official Catholic church historian, in his *Missions and Missionaries of California* [64]. However, Engelhardt's coverage was slanted to justify the Franciscan mission system whose effects, however noble in principle, were instrumental in the destruction of both the culture and population of about a quarter of the native societies. Bancroft's treatment stops at a point now nearly a century in the past. Sherburne F. Cook's three monographs *The Conflict Between the California Indian and White Civiliza-*

tion I, II, III, [37, 38, 39] most closely approach an adequate survey of the subject. These deal, in a far more scholarly and perceptive manner than Bancroft or Engelhardt, with the mission system and its effects (769–1834), the Mexican period (1821–1846), and the first twenty-five years of the American period (1846–1870); but here again, the last century of Indian history is not covered. Jack D. Forbes's *Native Americans of California and Nevada* [69] offers a compact summary of California Indian history, especially on relations with the federal government, and Edward Castillo's "The Impact of Euro-American Exploration and Settlement" [32] is an excellent review of the subject.

Native World View

For the period of *native* history, that is prehistory (from the original settlement of California some eleven or twelve thousand years ago to its discovery by Europeans in 1542), there is a voluminous and specialized literature. Robert F. Heizer and Albert B. Elsasser, *Bibliography of California Archaeology* [103] contains references to the literature of this precontact period. Useful guides to archaeological site surveys and excavations can be found in Martin A. Baumhoff and Elsasser, *Summary of Archaeological Survey and Excavation in California* [16] and Hal Eberhart, "Published Archaeological Sites and Surveys in Southern California" [60]. Fairly detailed summaries of California prehistory can be found in

Jesse D. Jennings and Edward Norbeck, *Prehistoric Man in the New World* [118] and Gordon R. Willey, *An Introduction to North American Archaeology, I.* [191].

The aboriginal, pre-White, cultural background of California Indians; the nearly infinite detail on ways of making a living; social customs, technology, material culture, and the like among the 105 main tribal groups, is best summarized in Kroeber's *Handbook of the Indians of California* [128] and *The California Indians: A Source Book* edited by Heizer and Mary A. Whipple [108], which contains fifty articles selected to provide a general introduction to the varieties of culture in the state. Stephen Powers's *Tribes of California* [157] is a tribe-by-tribe description of most of the main groups living north of the Tehachapi Mountains. Written in the early 1870s by an acute and sympathetic observer — a journalist — this volume stands not only as a solid record of native customs, but incidentally as a contemporary picture of what it was like to live as an Indian in California twenty-five years after the Gold Rush.

Two scientific series published by the University of California, University of California Publications in American Archaeology and Ethnology [177] and Anthropological Records [176], contain the largest collections of articles and monographs on tribal cultures. George Peter Murdock's *Ethnographic Bibliography of North America* as revised by Timothy J. O'Leary [151] is quite complete in its listing, by tribe, of articles and books on California Indians.

There are several ways in which anthropologists classify societies. Societies can be grouped into categories according to their basic economic pursuit (hunting–gathering, farming, stockbreeding, fishing); by culture type expressed in terms of culture areas; by level of technological development; or by language.

Linguistic classification is useful because it allows us to identify geographically separated (but historically related) languages which derive from a common ancestral speech. For California Indians, the first map of languages and tribes was that in Powers, *Tribes* [157], and was superseded by that in John W. Powell, "Indian Linguistic Families of North America" [156]. The basic map, compiled from the great body of information secured up to that date, is that in Kroeber, *Handbook;* this has been corrected on the basis of additional data in Heizer, *Languages, Territories and Names of California Indian Tribes* [94]. No scholar has attempted to write a historical survey of linguistic studies in California; the closest approximation is William Shipley, "California" [165]. This whole body of anthropological reportage is essential information for studies of culture change (acculturation) and provides basic knowledge about the operation of culture systems.

Acculturation studies among California Indians are rare. Why this kind of research has been neglected by anthropologists remains a puzzle. Some contributions to the subject are: F. J. Simoons, "Changes in Indian Life in the Clear Lake Area" [166]; E. R. Armsby and J. G.

Rockwell, "New Directions Among California Indians" [6]; Jaime de Angulo, "Indians in Overalls" [5]; Cook, *The Mechanism and Extent of Dietary Adaptation Among Certain Groups of California and Nevada Indians* [36]; C. Kasch, "The Yokayo Rancheria" [120]; Gordon MacGregor, "The Social and Economic Adjustment of the Indians of the Sacramento Jurisdiction of California" [144]; and Lowell John Bean, "Cultural Change in Cahuilla Religious and Political Leadership Patterns" [17].

One specialized form of acculturation study is the archaeological investigation and analysis of materials recovered from sites occupied by native peoples in the historical period. Studies of this sort include James J. F. Deetz, *Archaeological Investigations at La Purisima Mission* [53] and Heizer and John E. Mills, *The Four Ages of Tsurai* [105] which is a study of a single Yurok village at Trinidad Bay from the time of its discovery by Europeans in 1775 until its abandonment in 1916.

Some acculturation studies by linguists have shown how new culture traits adopted by Indians can be identified by their linguistic terms. Among such studies are: William Bright, *Animals of Acculturation in the California Indian Languages* [23]; William and Elizabeth Bright, "Spanish Words in Patwin" [24]; Robert L. Oswalt, "Russian Loan words in Southwestern Pomo" [154]; and William Shipley, "Spanish Elements in the Indigenous Languages of Central California" [164]. Kroeber's *California Place Names of Indian Origin* [126] illustrates the Indian influence on present-day toponomy; it is excellent, though incomplete.

Autobiographies of native people often illustrate the problems and processes of adjustment to living in two worlds. The most interesting example is Elizabeth Colson's *Autobiographies of Three Pomo Women* [33] recorded in 1941. Two particularly interesting autobiographies of members of the Yokuts tribe were recorded by Frank F. Latta in *Handbook of Yokuts Indians* [136]. A bibliography of sixteen additional Native Californian autobiographical accounts compiled by Karen Nissen is provided in Colson's *Autobiographies*. Forbes's "The Native American Experience in California History" [70] is a strong and perceptive statement on the social and psychological strength of traditional Indian culture, which still persists. The most intensive psychological study of any California tribe is provided by George Devereux, *Mohave Ethnopsychiatry and Suicide* [55]; it is difficult reading but extremely interesting in the detailed case histories and their analyses. There are no equally intensive studies for other tribes, but Erik H. Erikson's "Observations of the Yurok: Childhood and World Image" [65] gives us a Freudian's interpretation of a tribal personality quite different from that of the Mohave. Other attempts to define native thought patterns, values, and world view are: Thomas R. Garth, "Emphasis on Industriousness Among the Atsugewi" [72]; Walter Goldschmidt, "Ethics and the Structure of Society" [86], in which Yurok culture is skillfully and imaginatively compared to emerging European capitalism and the Protestant ethic; Dorothy Demetracopoulou Lee, "Notes on the Concept of Self Among the

Wintu Indians" [137]; Gertrude Toffelmeier and Katherine Luomela, "Dreams and Dream Interpretation of the Diegueno Indians" [173]; Raymond C. White, "The Luiseño Theory of Knowledge" [189]; and Bean, *Mukat's People* [18]. How men and women in Native California allocated those duties for which each was responsible is reviewed in the detailed study by Nona C. Willoughby, *Division of Labor Among the Indians of California* [192]. Heizer and Nissen in *The Human Sources of California Ethnography* [106] have compiled a list of the names, birthdates, and tribal affiliations of over two thousand Native Californians who have provided information to ethnographers and linguists.

The intimate connection between the physical features of the land and the occupant native peoples, a relationship often referred to as "ecological," is illustrated in Thomas T. Waterman, *Yurok Geography* [184], the most detailed native toponymic study ever carried out among California Indians. For central California, Samuel A. Barrett's *The Ethno-Geography of the Pomo and Neighboring Indians* [11] is very detailed; the closest parallel for southern California is William D. Strong, *Aboriginal Society in Southern California* [170].

Folklore and mythology were the means available to Indians for explaining how the world and what it held came to be that way. There is a tremendous literature on the subject, but collections of representative myths are scarce. Popular collections assembled and rewritten by untrained persons (usually motivated by a desire for profit) should be avoided — they are poorly done and often misleading. Edward W. Gifford and Gwendoline Harris Block, *Californian Indian Nights Entertainments* [84] is excellent, and it attempts to draw examples of the main types of tales from all regions of the state. Anna H. Gayton's more technical article, "Areal Affiliations of California Folktales" [74] traces the wider connections of California myth plots and includes a valuable bibliography on the subject. A monumental collection of the myths of one tribe is Barrett, *Pomo Myths* [13]. *Yurok Narratives* by Robert Spott, a Yurok, and Kroeber [167] contains myths with historical reference as well as "pure" myths. Other substantial tribal myth collections are by Roland B. Dixon, "Maidu Myths [57]; Julian H. Steward, *Myths of the Owens Valley Paiute* [168]; and Gayton and Stanley S. Newman, *Yokuts and Western Mono Myths* [75]. Of special value is Dorothy Demetracopoulou and Cora DuBois, "A Study of Wintu Mythology" [54], a large collection of tribal myths prefaced with a discussion of their literary aspects and their place in the culture.

Religion, with which myths are often but not always associated, is surveyed in Kroeber's *Handbook* [128]. The organized cult of northwestern California is described in detail in Kroeber and Gifford, *World Renewal: A Cult System of Native Northwest California* [132]. The central California Kuksu Cult is summarized in Kroeber, *Patwin* [129] and more amply described in Edwin M. Loeb's *The Western Kuksu Cult* [140] and *The Eastern Kuksu Cult* [141]. Creation myths and concepts are varied. Samples of such beliefs can be drawn from Angulo, "Pomo Creation Myth" [4]; John Peabody Harrington, "A Yuma Account of Origins" [90]; Loeb, "The Creator Concept Among the Indians of North Central California" [139]; and Waterman, "Analysis of the Mission Indian Creation Story" [183].

Material culture is a large subject. Barrett's *Material Aspects of Pomo Culture* [14] is a thorough inventory of the manufactures of one tribe, and his *Pomo Indian Basketry* [12] ably describes the textile processes and forms. Kroeber discussed California basket-making as a whole in "California Basketry and the Pomo" [124]. Some idea of the botanical and mineralogical knowledge of the California Indians can be gained from Ruth E. Merrill, *Plants Used in Basketry by the California Indians* [149] and Heizer and Adan E. Treganza, "Mines and Quarries of the Indians of California" [107]. The surprisingly wide network of trails and intertribal trade relations is presented by James T. Davis, *Trade Routes and Economic Exchange Among the Indians of California* [52].

Demography

Original population numbers and the decline in population resulting from White contact operating through changes in living patterns, diet, disease, and homicide since the first settlement in 1769 are topics covered by Cook in a series of monographs and a collection of essays: *The Aboriginal Population of the San Joaquin*

Valley [42]; *The Aboriginal Population of Alameda and Contra Costa Counties* [45]; *The Aboriginal Population of the North Coast of California* [44]; and *The Population of the California Indians, 1769–1970* [48]. This last work concludes that in late aboriginal times there were between 300,000 and 350,000 Indians living in California. This volume includes essays which consider the changing age distributions, degree of blood, and urban–rural distributions for the period 1769–1970. It stands as the considered conclusions of a scholar who, for forty years, was involved with California Indian demography. Separate studies of tribal or regional population numbers have been made by Herbert R. Harvey, "Population of the Cahuilla Indians" [91]; Alan K. Brown, *The Aboriginal Population of the Santa Barbara Channel* [25], a study of the Chumash in the discovery period; and Baumhoff, *The Ecological Determinants of Aboriginal California Populations* [15], a careful inquiry into the relation of food resources, especially acorns and salmon, to population densities. Official censuses are useless for determining Indian population until the Thirteenth Census of 1910, as Kroeber pointed out in his "California Indian Population About 1910" [130]. Cook's *Conflict Between California Indians and White Civilization, II* and *III* [38, 39] contains a population table running from 1832 and 1940, arranged by tribe, which is well documented and remains the best longitudinal study available. C. E. Kelsey, *Census of Non-Reservation California Indians, 1905–1906* [122] lists about 13,000 individuals by personal or family name and tribal group in addition to the 7,000 reservation Indians listed by Kroeber, "Population, 1910." This yields a total of 20,000 for the state in 1910, although the official federal census gives only a total of 13,000 Native Californians, as Dixon reported in his *Statistics of the Indian Population* [58].

The retention of Indian genetic strains (proportions of ancestral stocks) is considered in Cook's *Population of California Indians* [48] and in Kroeber and Heizer, "Continuity of Indian Population in California from 1770/1845 to 1955" [133], a study based on the California Roll of 1955. This study shows that, genetically speaking, there are very few truly extinct native groups, although in a cultural sense, most of these tribal societies no longer exist. Cook, "Racial Fusion Among California and Nevada Indians" [41] assesses the extent of genetic admixture among California Indians.*

The physical characteristics of California Indians and recognizable regional sub-types are fully presented in Gifford's *Californian Anthropometry* [82] and his "California Indian Types" [83] provides a helpful summary with fewer details. The photographs printed in Theodora Kroeber and Heizer, *Almost Ancestors* [134] and Gifford's *Anthropometry* show what California Indians looked like.

Native social organization is summarized in

---

*Cook outlined the sociology of this genetic dilution of Indian ancestry in the fourth volume of *Conflict*, subtitled *Trends in Marriage and Divorce Since 1850.* Ibero-Americana:24. Berkeley: University of California Press, 1943.

Goldschmidt, "Social Organization in Native California and the Origin of Clans" [85]. The nature and kinds of tribal organizations are discussed by Kroeber, *Two Papers on the Aboriginal Ethnography of California* [131]. In the second of these, he treats the "tribelet," the basic land-owning group of aboriginal times.

Indian–White Relations to 1870

European influence in California began in 1542 with the discovery by the Portuguese sea captain, Juan Rodriguez Cabrillo, the first European to die and be buried in what is now California. Cabrillo's journal, together with those of Cermeno in 1595 and Vizcaino in 1602, is published in Henry R. Wagner's *Spanish Voyages to the Northwest Coast of America in the Sixteenth Century* [180]. These journals contain the earliest descriptions of native peoples and cultures by European observers. In 1579 Sir Francis Drake spent five weeks in a still unidentified bay repairing his ship, *Golden Hinde,* and receiving visitors from the Coast Miwok tribe, who apparently took the English to be ghosts of the dead returned to earth. This incident is analyzed in Heizer, *Frances Drake and the California Indians, 1579* [93]. The first Spanish overland expedition to California was commanded by Gaspar de Portola in 1769. Father Juan Crespi's diary is perhaps the best of several journals kept of the expedition. It has been translated by Hubert Eugene Bolton under the title, *Fray Juan Crespi, Missionary Explorer on the Pacific Coast, 1769–1774* [21].

The series of twenty-one Franciscan missions established along the coast of California, from San Diego (est. 1769) to Sonoma (est. 1823), drew into its confines a total of 54,000 natives up to the time the missions were secularized in 1834 and the 15,000 surviving neophytes were released. Mortality in the missions, from disease and other factors, was very high as is demonstrated by Cook's careful study, *Population Trends Among the California Mission Indians* [35] and Jacob N. Bowman's year-by-year census of mission residents in "The Resident Neophytes (*Existentes*) of the California Missions" [22]. Ways in which the baptized Indian had to change his life in accordance with the mission regime can be seen in the statistical records and annual reports of the missions, summarized in Bancroft's *History* [9] and Cook's *Conflict, I* [37] as well as in descriptions on mission life recorded by European visitors, a list of whom is provided by Francis J. Weber, "The California Missions and Their Visitors" [187]. Of special interest are some accounts of mission life written, or dictated, by Indians who had been born in the missions. There are at least three such accounts: Pablo Tac's "Indian Life and Customs at Mission San Luis Rey" [172]; Lorenzo Asisara's narrative of life in Santa Cruz and other Costanoan missions published in Edward S. Harrison's *History of Santa Cruz County* [7]; and Julio Cesar's account of life in Mission San Luis Rey where he was born in 1824, which exists in a unique manuscript in the collection of the Bancroft Library [19]. Hugo Reid's *The Indians of Los Angeles County* [160], a collection of twenty-two letters originally published in the Los Angeles *Star* in 1852, is an authoritative description of tribal customs and mission life at San Gabriel written by a Scot who was married to a Gabrielino woman.

In 1812 the Spanish Secretary of Foreign Relations sent a questionnaire (*interrogatorio*) to each of the Franciscan missions in California with the aim of securing information on native practices and beliefs. The detailed replies have not been published in full under a single cover, but certain replies from individual missions have been translated and published by Maynard Geiger, O.F.M. in *Americas* [77, 78, 79, 80]; by Engelhardt, *Missions and Missionaries* [64]; by Heizer, *The Costanoan Indians* [96]; and in summary form by Kroeber, *A Mission Record of the California Indians* [125]. Aside from Father Geronimo Boscana's famous account of the religion of the Indians of Mission San Juan Capistrano (first published by Alfred Robinson, *Life in California* [162] and most recently by Henri and Paulette Reichlen, "Le Manuscrit Boscana de la Bibliothèque Nationale de Paris" [159]) the Franciscan missionaries, unlike the Jesuits, took no interest in writing descriptions of Indian customs. For this reason, the 1812 *Interrogatorio* replies are of particular importance in informing us about what and how much the missionaries really knew about the cultures of the native peoples, which they were so busily reshaping.

Bancroft was strongly critical of the "Indian policies" of the Franciscan order in the California missions; Engelhardt, *Missions and Missionaries* [64] defended it, as did Geiger, *The Life and Times of Fray Junipero Serra* [76].

Military expeditions sent out from the missions or *presidios* during the Spanish and Mexican periods are summarized in Bancroft, *History, I, II* [9]. Full translations of many of the official reports of these punitive forays have been published by Cook, *Colonial Expeditions to the Interior of California* [46, 47].

Despite the oppressive conditions which the Indians experienced in the missions, there were remarkably few revolts. The neophytes at San Diego Mission revolted in 1775, and the Colorado Mission was destroyed by the non-missionized Yumas in 1781. Details of these incidents appear in Bancroft, *History, I* [9]. A revolt of the missionized Chumash was short-lived, according to contemporary reports collected and published by Geiger, "Fray Antonio Ripoli's Description of the Chumash Revolt at Santa Barbara in 1824" [81].

The brief Mexican period, dating from the Mexican Revolution (1821) to the seizure of California by United States military forces (1846), was one in which Indians were freed from the missions, but impressed as peons in areas where there were large ranchos. Cook, *Conflict, II* [38] treats Indian–White relations during these times. Robinson, *Life* [162] describes the society of the times, and Cecil Alan Hutchinson, *Frontier Settlement in Mexican California* [111] gives very good coverage of the legal and social situation of Indians in the Mexican period.

Only two years after the end of the Mexican period, James Marshall's discovery of gold at Coloma on 24 January 1848 signaled the start of the Gold Rush. Within a year, tens of thousands of Whites came to California in search of the metal. The auriferous region lay in the Sierra Nevada and in other mountain ranges in California, an area that had, until 1848, remained in exclusive possession of the Indians — beyond the zone of White settlement. Almost overnight this whole region was overrun by White men seeking gold. An abrupt confrontation of miners and resident natives was inevitable. Conflict between the two groups was frequent, often intense, and always detrimental to the Indians, whose bows and arrows were pitted against the rifles and pistols of the miners.

The federal government attempted to enter into treaty relations with the Indians in the hope of establishing a series of reserved areas where they might be protected and instructed in agriculture and other useful pursuits. Three treaty commissioners appointed by President Millard Fillmore entered in 1851 and 1852 into eighteen treaty agreements with the California Indians, mostly in the gold mining region. The treaties and some of the background for them are presented in Heizer, *The Eighteen Unratified Treaties of 1851–1852 Between the California Indians and the United States Government* [95].* George

---

*Reports by the treaty commissioners appear in United States Congress, Senate. 1852. *Executive Documents,* No. 4 on Special Session Called March 4, 1852. Washington, D.C.: Government Printing Office. The official journal of Commissioner Redick McKee is included in this collection of documents.

Gibbs kept a second journal of the McKee expedition to northwestern California. This was published by Henry Rowe Schoolcraft in 1853 and more recently, with annotations, by Heizer, *George Gibb's Journal of Redick McKee's Expedition Through Northwestern California in 1851* [101]. Senators John C. Fremont and William McKendree Gwin of the newly admitted state of California exerted sufficient influence to cause the Senate to refuse to ratify the eighteen treaties. An account of this political jugglery appears in William H. Ellison, "Rejection of the California Indian Treaties" [62]. Marion Lydia Lathrop, "The Indian Campaigns of General M. G. Vallejo" [135] and Heizer and Thomas R. Hester, "Names and Locations of Some Ethnographic Patwin and Maidu Villages" [104] contain a series of unofficial treaties made between Mexican settlers or Anglo landholders and certain Indian groups in the period just before statehood.

Mass killings of Indians were a feature of the twenty years following the Gold Rush. Heizer, *Collected Documents on the Causes and Events in the Bloody Island Massacre of 1850* [99] contains not only the official Army reports but the testimony of other people, including Indians, relating to the particularly brutal massacre at Clear Lake. Heizer and Alan J. Almquist, *The Other Californians* [102] and Millard F. Hudson, "The Pauma Massacre" [110] contain brief discussions of other mass killings.

Although California was admitted to the Union in 1850 as a non-slaveholding state, the California legislature in 1850 enacted "An Act for the Government and Protection of Indians," a thinly disguised legalization of what can be termed, at worst, Indian slavery or at best, enforced bondage. The Act and some of its effects are treated in Heizer and Almquist, *The Other Californians.* The considerable number of Native Californians who were thus killed or enslaved proves with what little value those people were held in the eyes of contemporary "society."

In the absence of the hoped-for acceptance of the treaties and in view of the ever-worsening relations between Whites and Indians, the federal government decided in 1853 to establish a series of military reservations on which Indians could be gathered and where they could be protected by troops. A number of reservations were established, but some existed for only a few years. For details, see: Edward E. Dale, *The Indians of the Southwest* [51]; William H. Ellison, "The Federal Indian Policy in California, 1846–1860" [61]; and Alban W. Hoopes, *Indian Affairs and Their Administration* [109]. Dishonesty among reservation Indian Agents was investigated by John Ross Browne, "The Coast Rangers, II: The Indian Reservations" [26]. *The Annual Reports of the Commissioner of Indian Affairs* [3] from 1852 and following years contain official reports of Indian agents on reservations. Letters from army officers in charge of troop detachments assigned to reservations are printed in Heizer, *The Destruction of the California Indians* [97].*

---

*The richest printed source of these letters and similar documents is United States, War Department. 1880–1901. 70 vols. in 128. *The War of the Rebellion: A Compilation of the Official Records of the Union and Confederate Armies . . .* Washington, D.C.: Government Printing Office.

Other — and unofficial — sources for the history of Indian–White relations from 1850 and following are newspaper accounts. These, inevitably, concentrate on "newsworthy" events: fights between two individuals or military expeditions against Indians in retaliation for some, generally imaginary, "atrocity"; Indians arrested for breaking hunting or fishing regulations or possessing firearms or whiskey; Indians being evicted from long-occupied villages, now claimed by some White land-holder who did not want "squatters" on his property; obituary articles on some aged and locally well known Indian; performance of some large ceremony in a nearby Indian village; reports on miserable conditions under which non-reservation Indians were living; and so on. It would be possible to draw from such information a reasonably clear picture of local attitudes towards Indians and to determine how the Indians were reacting to these attitudes. Although such an examination would require considerable time spent plodding through a dozen selected newspaper files for the last century, this is probably the only way to recover the facts of what is the otherwise unrecorded history of the non-reservation Indians: the descendants of those persons who had survived missionization, Mexican peonage, the Gold Rush, indenture, the reservation round-ups; people who were landless, but who had managed to survive on the fringes of White civilization in out-of-the-way spots where their presence did not interfere with farming and where they were socially unobtrusive. A published collection of 188 such newspaper articles on Indian–White relations dating from 1851 to 1866 can be found in Heizer, *They Were Only Diggers* [100]. Cook, *The Conflict of the California Indians and White Civilization, III* [39] relies heavily on newspaper reports for an analysis of relations between the two peoples in the period 1848 to 1870.

One reaction to White domination was Indian rebellion, and from 1850 to 1870 the Indians occasionally fought back against White brutality and encroachment. These so-called Indian Wars were infrequent, partly because of the overwhelmingly superior weaponry of the miners and regular military forces and partly because the Indians were not able to combine tribal forces, arm them, and train them into effective fighting units. Anthony J. Bledsoe, *Indian Wars in the Northwest* [20] reviews some of these one-sided conflicts which the Indians almost always lost badly. The last Indian uprising in Southern California occurred in 1851. It is summarized in William E. Evans, "The Garra Uprising" [66]; Noel M. Loomis, "The Garra Uprising of 1851" [142]; and is considered in greatest detail in George H. Phillips, *Chiefs and Challengers* [155]. The Indians also lost the Modoc War of the early 1870s, but they did succeed in inflicting heavy casualties on the seasoned United States Army troops who opposed them. This conflict is treated in Keith A. Murray, *The Modocs and their War* [150]; Jeff C. Riddle, *The Indian History of the Modoc War* [161], written by a half-Modoc who was nine years old when the war started; and Richard H. Dillon, *Burnt-Out Fires* [56].

Another response to conquest was nativistic religious movements. The earliest of these — still within the mission period — was one which occurred in the Santa Barbara area. The few known details on this incident are given in Heizer, "A California Messianic Movement of 1801 Among the Chumash" [92]. The Ghost Dance of 1870 in California is fully treated in DuBois, *The 1870 Ghost Dance* [59] and in Gayton, *The Ghost Dance of 1870 in South-Central California* [76]. Blends of the old pre-White Kuksu Cult and the Ghost Dance survive in the form of the Maru Cult, practiced by the Pomo. This is discussed in Clement Woodward Meighan and Francis A. Riddell, *The Maru Cult of the Pomo Indians* [147]; Clinton Hart Merriam, "The Expulsion of Sahte" [148]; and Birbeck Wilson, *Ukiah Valley Pomo Religious Life* [193]. Among the Mission Indians of Southern California some old religious beliefs and practices have been preserved, although in altered form as a result of two centuries of acculturation as shown by Bean, "Cultural Change in Cahuilla Religious and Political Leadership Patterns" [17] and Raymond C. White, *Luiseño Social Organization* [190]. In northwestern California the Indian Shaker Church has found adherents. The situation is described by Homer G. Barnett, *Indian Shakers* [10]; Dale Valory, "The Focus of Indian Shaker Healing" [178]; and Richard A. Gould and Paul Furukawa, "Aspects of Ceremonial Life Among the Indian Shakers of Smith River, California" [88].

The Reservation Period and Urbanization

By about 1870, early in President Grant's administration, the federal government acceded to the need to ameliorate the pitiable condition of the Indians of Southern California. The Indians and Whites, still hostile, had largely stopped fighting, and the country seemed sated with bloodshed by the conclusion of the Civil War. General John Baillie McIntosh, appointed Superintendent of Indian Affairs in California, in 1870 established the reservations at Pala and Pasqual, but violent protests from local White residents succeeded in forcing Grant to rescind his executive order the next year. New federal regulations which prohibited Army officers from holding civil office by either election or appointment led Grant to institute the so-called Quaker Policy, under which churches were invited to nominate Indian agents. This procedure met with limited success and it was abandoned within ten years. The reason for the failure seems to have been that high-minded preachers were ineffective administrators of their Indian wards, who were under strong pressure from Whites both from inside and outside the reservations. The Pala and San Pasqual affair aroused the public conscience, and in 1873 John G. Ames was sent as a special agent to investigate and report on the condition of the "Mission Indians." The "Report of Special Agent John G. Ames on the Condition of the Mission Indians" [3] attracted wide public attention. When it was followed by the *Report of Chas. A. Wetmore, Special U.S. Commissioner to the Mission Indians* [188], President Grant responded in 1875 by establishing nine reservations, and another six the next year. Helen Hunt Jackson's *A Century of Dishonor* [116] put further details of the Mission Indians' misery before a wide audience, and in 1882, the year after its publication, Jackson and Abbot Kinney were appointed as special agents in order to report further on conditions — appointments that resulted in their *Report on Condition and Needs of the Mission Indians of California* [117]. Also important in providing contemporary information on the condition of both landed and landless Indians of California are Kelsey's *Report of the Special Agent for California Indians to the Commissioner of Indian Affairs, March 21, 1906* [121] and Imre Sutton's survey of allotment land in Southern California, "Private Property in Land Among Reservation Indians in Southern California." [171] Further details of federal concern with the Mission Indians appear in Dale, *Indians of the Southwest* [51]. Reports of the living conditions and locations of the Indian reservations or allotment lands, almost one hundred years after Grant's initial efforts to improve them, appear in *Report of the California Senate Interim Committee on California Indian Affairs* [30] and *Report of the State Advisory Commission on Indian Affairs* [29]. These surveys contain important data, as well as large maps showing the location of the 117 parcels of Indian Trust

Lands in California constituting a total of 593,904 acres. This sounds like a considerable land holding — it is in terms of surface area — but most of it is barren, rocky, waterless, and useless land. If, however, the tempo of population increase in California continues at the same rate it has for the last thirty years, the Indian Trust Lands will some day become valuable real estate.

Proposed federal termination of services in behalf of Indians (the so-called Rancheria Act, 27 Stat. 619, amended in 78 Stat. 390 of 1958) is in the lethargic process of being put into action. Progress is slow and difficult because of the State's reluctance to assume responsibility for Indian Affairs, and there remain problems about who will provide the necessary funds for Indian welfare, as well as how Indian land title shall be guaranteed. Background on this complex matter can be found in *California Rancheria Task Force Report* of the Bureau of Indian Affairs [174]; *An Explanation of Termination* by the California Legal Services [28]; and *Report of the State Advisory Commission on Indian Affairs* [29].

The establishment of a boarding school on Tule River Reservation in 1881 marked the formal beginning of Indian education in California. A number of other schools on other reservations followed. The founding dates, attendance records, and other relevant information are available in the *Annual Reports of the Commissioner of Indian Affairs* [3]. Since 1917, the Bureau of Indian Affairs has contracted with the State Department of Education for the State to provide public schooling for

Native Californians. The *California State Senate Interim Committee* report [30], the *California State Advisory Commission* report [29], and Forbes, *California Indian Education* [71] contain recent information on Indian education.

No satisfactory data on Indian employment and education exist for the last century. Ernest B. Webb, *American Indians of California* [186] provides a careful compilation of data drawn from the 1960 census, specifying known information on educational attainment, employment, income, urban/rural population distribution, and family size. Cook, "Migration and Urbanization of the Indians of California" [40] analyzes the data recorded for the 23,542 Indians listed in the special census of 1928, predicting, correctly, that the percentage of urban Indians would increase. This percentage rose from thirteen in 1928 to fifty-three in 1960.

Indians and the Law

The legal history of the California Indian is better documented than the economic and demographic. A suit against the federal government allowed by the California Indians Jurisdiction Act of 1928 in the Court of Claims for compensation (Case K-344), mainly in satisfaction of grievances resulting from the Senate's refusal to ratify the eighteen treaties of 1851 to 1852, led to a favorable decision in 1942 bringing in a settlement of $5,025,000. Kenneth M. Johnson, *K-344, or the Indians of California, vs. the United States* [119] and Robert W. Kenny, *History and Proposed Settlement, Claims of California Indians* [123] summarize the history of the case. The Indian Claims Commission Act of 1946 (H.R. 4497) allowed a number of suits. The major one for California, Docket 31/37 was settled in favor of the Indian plaintiffs for $29,100,000 in 1968. No full account of this legal process has been written, but some information can be found in Nancy Oestreich Lurie, "The Indian Claims Commission Act" [143] and Omer C. Stewart, "Kroeber and the Indian Claims Commission Cases" [169].

The Indian as subject to state civil and criminal codes and federal statutes is a complex matter in California, as everywhere. For general background on federal regulations and policy, the reader is referred to Theodore H. Haas, "The Legal Aspects of Indian Affairs from 1887 to 1957" [89]; Wilcomb E. Washburn, *Red Man's Land/White Man's Law* [181]; and Washburn, *The American Indian and the United States* [182]. The basic specific reference to California Indians is Chauncey S. Goodrich, "The Legal Status of the California Indian" [87]. Heizer and Almquist, *Other Californians* [102] discusses the restrictive legislation of an earlier time on Indians' rights to schooling, land ownership, possession of firearms, voting, buying liquor, and the like. F. F. Fernandez, "Except a California Indian: A Study in Legal Discrimination" [68] is also useful. The Committee on Indian Affairs of the United States House of Representatives, "Reservation Courts of Indian Offenses" [175] contains printed testimony of Committee hearings on reservation legal proceedings in California.

For the first twenty years of government control, the Indian occasionally fought back against White brutality and encroachment, but these efforts were seen to be ineffective and were abandoned as useless. In the 1880s Indian welfare organizations, formed and led by Whites, took up the cause of improving the living conditions of Indians. Some of these organizations were short-lived; others remained active for relatively long periods. Most such groups published newsletters, but files of these are rare and usually incomplete. Examples of these newsletters include: *The Indian Sentinel,* distributed by the Bureau of Catholic Indian Missions [27]; *Annual Reports of the Executive Committee of the Indian Rights Association* [113]; *Indian Truth,* distributed by the Indian Rights Association [114]; *California Indian Herald,* issued by the Indian Board of Cooperation [112]; the Northern California Indian Association's *Newsletter* [152]; and the Sequoyah League's *Bulletin* [163]. In addition, the Commonwealth Club of California had, for a period in the mid-1920s, an active Section on Indian Affairs, as illustrated by Charles de Young Elkus, "Indians in California" [63]. In the 1950s, the American Friends Service Committee sent a field worker, Frank Quinn, to visit the reservations of northern California to discuss the proposed federal termination project with the residents. His booklet, *Indians of California, Past and Present* [158] is sound and informative.

From the 1920s, Indians have formed their own political organizations, for example, the Mission Indian Federation, the Northern California Brotherhood of Indians, the Inter-Tribal Council of California (which publishes *The Tribal Spokesman* [115]), the California League for American Indians, and the Council of California Indians. George E. Fay has compiled in *Charters, Constitutions and By-laws of the Indian Tribes of North America* [67] forty-two separate corporate charters, articles of association, and constitutions of California tribal groups. More recently, the American Indian Historical Society, which publishes a journal, *The Indian Historian* [1], a monthly newspaper, *Wassaja* [2], as well as books and a children's magazine, has served as a media outlet for Native Californian opinion. There is a great need for the energy of some scholar to compile a list of Indian welfare organizations, their period of activity, and where their publications (usually newsletters) are available for reference.

Much recent Indian political activity has taken the form of nationalism. This movement is best known for the occupation of Alcatraz Island from November 1969 to April 1971. No full account of this struggle to gain possession of the abandoned federal property has been written, but the essential story is described in Rupert Costo, "Alcatraz" [49]; Ray March, "On the 40th Day of the Indian Occupation of Alcatraz Island" [146]; and Richard Oaks, "Alcatraz is Not an Island" [153]. A great many documentary records, mostly concerning legal proceedings, no doubt exist, but day-by-day development of the Alcatraz occupation can best be seen in the reporters' accounts of such daily newspapers as the San Francisco *Chronicle*. Two films document the Pit River Struggle, the 1970 attempt by the Pit River tribe to occupy lands owned by the Pacific Gas and Electric Company. These are George Ballis, "The Dispossessed" [8] and Lee Callister and W. J. Carrol, "Forty-seven Cents" [31].

Other signs of and aids to the revitalization process of revival and maintenance of traditional Indian values and knowledge are the new Native American Studies programs, established in 1969 on the major compuses of the University of California and in some of the state colleges. These have generally prospered and their growth, while slow, has been steady. At the Davis campus of the University of California, a special school, Deganiwidah–Quetzalcoatl University has been in operation since 1970, and now offers a variety of courses on Native American history and culture. The Native American Studies programs in California are encouraging indications of continued interest in Native Californian history.

Memories, progressively dimmer, of the old, original native ways of life survived among some groups in California until about 1940. By that date the ethnographic record was as nearly complete as it was ever to be. That voluminous record, which is barely sampled here, is in need of reassessment in terms of how much of it needs reinterpretation in the light of the Indian experience from the time of first Spanish settlement. What this means is the application of ethnohistoric analysis where the ethnographic record and the documented history of events are combined. Thus far no person has attempted to do this, and when it is done, a new and more accurate and meaningful history of Native Californians will result.

Recommended Works

For the Beginner

[29]   California State Advisory Commission on Indian Affairs.

[37, 38,
39]   Sherburne F. Cook, *The Conflict of the California Indians and White Civilization, I, II,* and *III.*

[102]   Robert F. Heizer and Alan J. Almquist, *The Other Californians.*

[108]   Robert F. Heizer and Mary A. Whipple, eds., *The California Indians.*

[128]   Alfred L. Kroeber, *Handbook of the Indians of California.*

For a Basic Library Collection

[9]   Hubert H. Bancroft, *History of California.*

[18]   Lowell J. Bean, *Mukat's People.*

[33]   Elizabeth Colson, *Autobiographies of Three Pomo Women.*

[48]   Sherburne F. Cook, *The Population of the California Indians, 1769–1970.*

[51]   Everett E. Dale, *The Indians of the Southwest.*

[56]   Richard H. Dillon, *Burnt-Out Fires.*

[69]   Jack D. Forbes, *Native Americans of California and Nevada.*

[84]   Edward W. Gifford and Gwendoline H. Block, *Californian Indian Nights Entertainment.*

[87]   Chauncey S. Goodrich, "The Legal Status of the California Indian."

[116] Helen Hunt Jackson, *A Century of Dishonor.* Alfred L. Kroeber.

[128] *Handbook of the Indians of California.* *Two Papers on the Aboriginal Ethnography of California.*

[134] Theodora Kroeber and Robert F. Heizer, *Almost Ancestors.*

[155] George H. Phillips, *Chiefs and Challengers.*

[157] Stephen Powers, *Tribes of California.*

[167] Robert Spott and Alfred L. Kroeber, *Yurok Narratives.*

[192] Nona C. Willoughby, *Division of Labor Among the Indians of California.*

Bibliographical List

*Denotes items suitable for secondary school students

American Indian Historical Society.

[1]   *The Indian Historian.* 1964–   . San Francisco.

[2]   *Wassaja.* 1973–   . San Francisco.

*[3]   Ames, John Griffiths. 1874. "Report of Special

Agent John G. Ames in Regard to the Condition of the Mission Indians of California, with Recommendations." In *Annual Report of the Commissioner of Indian Affairs to the Secretary of the Interior for the Year 1873,* Appendix A, pp. 29–40. Washington, D.C.: Government Printing Office. (Reprinted in *Reprints of Various Papers on California Archaeology, Ethnology and Indian History,* comp. and ed. Robert F. Heizer, pp. 70–89. Berkeley: University of California Archaeological Research Facility, Department of Anthropology, 1973.) [The *Reports* cover the period 1824–1932. Until 1849, Indian affairs were subordinate to the War Department; the office of commissioner was created by Congress in 1832.]

Angulo, Jaime de.

[4]   1935. "Pomo Creation Myth." *Journal of American Folklore* 48:203–62.

[5]   1950. "Indians in Overalls." *Hudson Review* 3:327–77.

[6]   Armsby, E. R. and Rockwell, J. G. 1948. "New Directions Among California Indians." *The American Indian* (Sept.) 4:12–23.

*[7]   Asisara, Lorenzo. 1892. "Personal Narrative of a Former Neophyte Born at Santa Cruz Mission in 1819." In *History of Santa Cruz County, Cali-*

fornia, Edmund Sanford Harrison, pp. 45–48. San Francisco: Pacific Press Pub. Co. [for the author].

*[8]   Ballis, George, prod. and dir. n.d. "The Dispossessed." [Film, 16 mm] Berkeley: University of California Extension Media Center. [Listed in *EMC* catalogue as No. 9015.]

[9]   Bancroft, Hubert Howe. 1884–90. *History of California.* 7 vols. San Francisco: The History Co.

[10]   Barnett, Homer Garner. 1967. *Indian Shakers; A Messianic Cult of the Pacific Northwest.* Carbondale: University of Southern Illinois Press.

Barrett, Samuel Alfred.

*[11]   1908. *The Ethno-Geography of the Pomo and Neighboring Indians.* University of California Publications in American Archaeology and Ethnology: 6, pt. 1, pp. 1–332. Berkeley: University of California Press.

*[12]   1908. *Pomo Indian Basketry.* University of California Publications in American Archaeology and Ethnology:7, pt. 3, pp. 133–308. Berkeley: University of California Press.

*[13]   1933. *Pomo Myths.* Bulletin of the Public Museum of the City of Milwaukee:15. Milwaukee, Wisc.: The Trustees.

*[14]   1952. *Material Aspects of Pomo Culture.* 2 vols. Bulletin of the Public Museum of the City of Milwaukee:20. Milwaukee, Wisc.: The Trustees.

[15]   Baumhoff, Martin A. 1956. *Ecological Determinants of Aboriginal California Population.* University of California Publications in American Archaeology and Ethnology:49, pt. 2, pp. 155–236. Berkeley: University of California Press.

[16]   Baumhoff, Martin A. and Elsasser, Albert B. 1956. *Summary of Archaeological Survey and Excavation in California.* Reports of the University of California Archaeological Survey:33. Berkeley: University of California, Department of Anthropology.

Bean, Lowell John.

[17]   1964. "Cultural Change in Cahuilla Religious and Political Leadership Patterns." In *Cultural Change and Stability. Essays in Memory of Olive Ruth Barker and George C. Barker,* ed. Ralph Leon Beals, pp. 1–10. Los Angeles: University of California, Department of Anthropology.

[18]   1972. *Mukat's People: The Cahuilla Indians of Southern California.* Berkeley: University of California Press.

[19]   Berkeley. University of California, Bancroft Library. 1879. "Cosas de Indios de California." [Manuscript] Julio Cesar.

[20]   Bledsoe, Anthony Jennings. 1885. *Indian Wars in the Northwest: A California Sketch*. San Francisco: Bacon and Co.

[21]   Bolton, Herbert Eugene. 1927. *Fray Juan Crespi, Missionary Explorer on the Pacific Cost, 1769–1774*. Berkeley: University of California Press.

[22]   Bowman, Jacob N. 1958. "The Resident Neophytes *(Existentes)* of the California Missions, 1769–1834." *Historical Society of Southern California Quarterly* 40:138–48.

[23]   Bright, William. 1960. *Animals of Acculturation in the California Indian Languages*. University of California Publications in Linguistics:4, pt. 4, pp. 214–46. Berkeley: University of California Press.

[24]   Bright, William and Bright, Elizabeth. 1959. "Spanish Words in Patwin." *Romance Philology* (Nov.) 13:161–64.

[25]   Brown, Alan K. 1967. *The Aboriginal Population of the Santa Barbara Channel*. University of California Archaeological Survey Reports:69. Berkeley: University of California, Department of Anthropology.

*[26]   Browne, John Ross. 1861. "The Coast Rangers, A Chronicle of Events in California, II: The Indian Reservations." *Harper's New Monthly Magazine* 23:306–16.

[27]   Bureau of Catholic Indian Missions. *The Indian Sentinel.* 1902/03–   . Washington, D.C.

[28]   California Indian Legal Services, Inc. 1968. *An Explanation of Termination.* Berkeley: California Indian Legal Services, Inc.

[29]   California State Senate Advisory Commission on Indian Affairs. 1966. *Progress Report to the Governor and the Legislature on Indians in Rural and Reservation Areas.* Sacramento: State Printing Office.

[30]   California State Senate Interim Committee on California Indian Affairs. 1955. *Progress Report to the Legislature.* Sacramento: State Printing Office.

[31]   Callister, Lee and Carrol, W. J., prods. 1973. "Forty-seven Cents." [Film, 16 mm] Berkeley: University of California Extension Media Center.

*[32]   Castillo, Edward. Forthcoming. "The Impact of Euro-American Exploration and Settlement on the Indians of California." In *Handbook of North American Indians,* gen. ed. William C. Sturtevant. Washington, D.C.: Smithsonian Institution.

*[33]   Colson, Elizabeth. 1974. *Autobiographies of Three Pomo Women.* Berkeley: University of California Archaeological Research Facility, Department of Anthropology.

Cook, Sherburne Friend.
*[34]   1939. "Smallpox in Spanish and Mexican California, 1770–1845." *Bulletin of the History of Medicine* 7:153–91.

[35]   1940. *Population Trends Among the California Mission Indians.* Ibero-Americana:17. Berkeley: University of California Press.

[36]   1941. *The Mechanism and Extent of Dietary Adaptation Among Certain Groups of California and Nevada Indians.* Ibero-Americana:18. Berkeley: University of California Press.

*[37]   1943. *The Conflict Between the California Indian and White Civilization: I. The Indian Versus the Spanish Mission.* Ibero-Americana:21. Berkeley: University of California Press.

[38]   1943. *The Conflict Between the California Indian and White Civilization: II. The Physical And Demographic Reaction of Nonmission Indians in Colonial and Provincial California.* Ibero-Americana:22. Berkeley: University of California Press.

*[39]   1943. *The Conflict Between the California Indian and White Civilization: III. The American Invasion,*

1848–1870. Ibero-Americana:23. Berkeley: University of California Press.

[40]   1943. "Migration and Urbanization of the Indians of California." *Human Biology* 15:33–45.

[41]   1943. "Racial Fusion Among the California and Nevada Indians." *Human Biology* 15:153–65.

[42]   1955. *The Aboriginal Population of the San Joaquin Valley, California.* Anthropological Records:16, pt. 2, pp. 31–80. Berkeley: University of California Press.

[43]   1955. *The Epidemic of 1830–1833 in California and Oregon.* University of California Publications in American Archaeology and Ethnology:43, pt. 3, pp. 303–26. Berkeley: University of California Press.

[44]   1956. *The Aboriginal Population of the North Coast of California.* Anthropological Records:16, pt. 3, pp. 81–129. Berkeley: University of California Press.

[45]   1957. *The Aboriginal Population of Alameda and Contra Costa Counties, California.* Anthropological Records:16, pt. 4, pp. 131–55. Berkeley: University of California Press.

*[46]   1960. *Colonial Expeditions to the Interior of California: Central Valley, 1800–1820.* Anthropol-

ogical Records:16, pt. 6, pp. 239–92. Berkeley: University of California Press.

[47] 1962. *Expeditions to the Interior of California: Central Valley, 1820–1840.* Anthropological Records:20, pt. 5, pp. 151–214. Berkeley: University of California Press.

[48] 1976. *The Population of the California Indians, 1769–1970.* Berkeley: University of California Press.

[49] Costo, Rupert. 1970. "Alcatraz." *The Indian Historian* (Winter) 3:4–12.

[50] Cowan, Robert Ernest and Cowan, Robert Granniss, comps. 1933. *A Bibliography of the History of California, 1510–1930.* San Francisco: J. H. Nash.

*[51] Dale, Edward Everett. 1949. *The Indians of the Southwest; A Century of Development Under the United States.* Norman: University of Oklahoma Press.

*[52] Davis, James T. 1961 *Trade Routes and Economic Exchange Among the Indians of California.* Reports of the University of California Archaeological Survey:54. Berkeley: University of California, Department of Anthropology. (Reprinted, Ballena Press Publications in Archaeology, Ethnology and History:3, ed. Robert F. Heizer, Ramona, Calif.: Ballena Press, 1974.)

[53]   Deetz, James J. F. 1963. *Archaeological Investigations at La Purisima Mission.* Archaeological Survey Annual Report for 1962–1963. Los Angeles: University of California, Department of Anthropology and Sociology.

*[54]   Demetracopoulou, Dorothy and DuBois, Cora. 1932. "A Study of Wintu Mythology." *Journal of American Folklore* 45:373–500.

[55]   Devereux, George. 1961. *Mohave Ethnopsychiatry and Suicide: The Psychiatric Knowledge and the Psychic Disturbances of an Indian Tribe.* Smithsonian Institution, Bureau of American Ethnology, Bulletin:175. Washington, D.C.: U. S. Government Printing Office.

*[56]   Dillon, Richard H. 1973. *Burnt-Out Fires: California's Indian Modoc War.* Englewood Cliffs, N.J.: Prentice-Hall.

Dixon, Roland Burrage.

[57]   1902. "Maidu Myths." *Bulletin of the American Museum of Natural History* 17:33–118.

[58]   1910. *Statistics of the Indian Population — Number, Tribes, Sex, Age, Fecundity, and Vitality.* Special Publication of the Thirteenth Census of the United States, Bureau of the Census. Washington, D.C.: Government Printing Office.

[59]   DuBois, Cora Alice. 1939. *The 1870 Ghost Dance.*

Anthropological Records:3, pt. 1, pp. 1–151. Berkeley: University of California Press.

[60] Eberhart, Harold Hal. 1970. "Published Archaeological Sites and Surveys in Southern California." *Newsletter of the Archaeological Survey Association of Southern California* (Fall/Winter) 17:4–21.

Ellison, William Henry.

*[61] 1922. "The Federal Indian Policy in California, 1846–1860." *Mississippi Valley Historical Review* 9:37–67.

*[62] 1925. "Rejection of California Indian Treaties: A Study in Local Influence on National Policy." *Grizzly Bear* 36: (May no. 217), pp. 4–5; (June, no. 218), pp. 4, 5, and 7; (July no. 219), pp. 6–7.

[63] Elkus, Charles de Young, chmn. 1926. "Indians in California." *Transactions of the Commonwealth Club of California* vol. 21, no. 3, pp. 103–31. Also appears as *The Commonwealth, Part II* vol. 2, no. 3. [Elkus provided an introduction and summation for this collection of short pieces.]

[64] Engelhardt, Zephyrin. 1929. *The Missions and Missionaries of California.* 2 vols. 2nd ed. Volume 2: *Upper California.* Santa Barbara: Mission Santa Barbara.

[65] Erikson, Eric Homburger. 1943. *Observations on*

the Yurok: Childhood and World Image. University of California Publications in American Archaeology and Ethnology:35, pt. 20, pp. 257–302. Berkeley: University of California Press.

[66]   Evans, William E. 1966. "The Garra Uprising: Conflict Between San Diego Indians and Settlers in 1851." *California Historical Society Quarterly* 45:339–49.

[67]   Fay, George Emory, comp. and ed. 1970. *Charters, Constitutions and By-Laws of the Indian Tribes of North America. Parts VII, VIII: The Indian Tribes of California.* Colorado State College, Museum of Anthropology, Occasional Publications in Anthropology, Ethnology Series:7 and 8. Greeley: Colorado State College, Museum of Anthropology.

*[68]   Fernandez, F. F. 1968. "Except a California Indian: A Study in Legal Discrimination." *Southern California Quarterly* 50:161–76.

Forbes, Jack D.

*[69]   1969. *Native Americans of California and Nevada.* Healdsburg, Calif.: Naturegraph Pub.

[70]   1971. "The Native American Experience in California History." *California Historical Quarterly* 50:234–42.

[71]   Forbes, Jack D., ed. 1967. *California Indian Edu-cation: Report of the First All Indian Statewide Con ference on California Indian Education.* Modesto, Calif.: Ad Hoc Committee on California Indian Education.

[72]   Garth, Thomas Russell. 1945. "Emphasis on In-dustriousness Among the Atsugewi." *American Anthropologist* 47:554–66.

Gayton, Anna Hadwick.

[73]   1930. *The Ghost Dance of 1870 in South-Central California.* University of California Publications in American Archaeology and Ethnology:28, pt. 3, pp. 57–82. Berkeley: University of California Press.

[74]   1935. "Areal Affiliations of California Folk-tales." *American Anthropologist* 37:582–99.

[75]   Gayton, Anna Hadwick and Newman, Stanley Stewart. 1940. *Yokuts and Western Mono Myths.* Anthropological Records:5, pt. 1, pp. 1–109. Berkeley: University of California Press.

[76]   Geiger, Maynard, J. 1959. *The Life and Times of Fray Junipero Serra, O.F.M.; or The Man Who Never Turned Back, 1713–1784, A Biography.* Washington, D.C.: Academy of American Fran-ciscan History.

Geiger, Maynard, J., ed. and trans.

[77] 1949. "Reply of the Mission San Diego to the Questionnaire of the Spanish Government in 1812 Concerning the Native Culture of the California Mission Indians." *Americas* 5:474–90.

[78] 1950. "Reply of the Mission San Carlos Borromeo to the Questionnaire of the Spanish Government in 1812 Concerning the Native Culture of the California Mission Indians." *Americas* 6:467–86.

[79] 1953. "Reply of the Mission San Antonio to the Questionnaire of the Spanish Government in 1812 Concerning the Native Culture of the California Mission Indians." *Americas* 10:211–27.

[80] 1955. "Reply of the Mission San Gabriel to the Questionnaire of the Spanish Government in 1812 Concerning the Native Culture of the California Mission Indians." *Americas* 12:77–84.

[81] 1970. "Fray Antonio Ripoll's Description of the Chumash Revolt at Santa Barbara in 1824." *Southern California Quarterly* 52:345–64.

Gifford, Edward Winslow.

[82] 1926. *Californian Anthropometry*. University of California Publications in American Archaeology and Ethnology:22, pt. 2, pp. 217–390. Berkeley: University of California Press.

[83]   1926. "California Indian Types." *Natural History* 26:50 60.

*[84]   Gifford, Edward Winslow and Block, Gwendoline Harris, comps. 1930. *Californian Indian Nights Entertainments; Stories of the Creation of the World, of Man, of Fire, of the Sun, of Thunder, etc.; of Coyote, the Land of the Dead, the Sky Land, Monsters, Animal People, etc.* Glendale, Calif.: The Arthur H. Clark Co.

         Goldschmidt, Walter.

[85]   1948. "Social Organization in Native California and the Origin of Clans." *American Anthropologist* 50:444–56.

[86]   1951. "Ethics and the Structure of Society." *American Anthropologist* 53:506–24.

[87]   Goodrich, Chauncey Shafter. 1926. "The Legal Status of the California Indian." *California Law Review* 14:83–100; 157–87.

[88]   Gould, Richard A. and Furukawa, Paul. 1964. "Aspects of Ceremonial Life Among the Indian Shakers of Smith River, California." *Kroeber Anthropological Society Papers* 31:51–67.

*[89]   Hass, Theodore H. 1957. "The Legal Aspects of Indian Affairs from 1887 to 1957." *Annals of the American Academy of Political and Social Science* 311:12–22.

[90]   Harrington, John Peabody. 1908. "A Yuma Account of Origins." *Journal of American Folklore* 21:324–48.

[91]   Harvey, Herbert R. 1967. "Population of the Cahuilla Indians: Decline and Its Causes." *Eugenics Quarterly* 14:185–98.

Heizer, Robert Fleming.

[92]   1941. "A California Messianic Movement of 1801 Among the Chumash." *American Anthropologist* 43:128–29.

*[93]   1947. *Francis Drake and the California Indians, 1579*. University of California Publications in American Archaeology and Ethnology:42, pt. 3, pp. 251–301. Berkeley: University of California Press. (Reprinted, with additional discussion, in *Elizabethan California* . . . pp. 49–95. Ramona, Calif.: Ballena Press, 1975.)

[94]   1966. *Languages, Territories, and Names of California Indian Tribes*. Berkeley: University of California Press.

*[95]   1972. *The Eighteen Unratified Treaties of 1851– 1852 Between the California Indians and the United States Government*. Berkeley: University of California Archaeological Research Facility, Department of Anthropology.

[96]   1974. *The Costanoan Indians*. California History

Center, Local History Studies:18. Cupertino, Calif.: De Anza College.

*[97]   1974. *The Destruction of the California Indians.* Salt Lake City: Peregrine Pub.

Heizer, Robert Fleming, comp.

[98]   1969. *Catalogue of the C. Hart Merriam Collection of Data Concerning California Tribes and Other American Indians.* Berkeley: University of California Archaeological Research Facility, Department of Anthropology.

*[99]   1974. *Collected Documents on the Causes and Events in the Bloody Island Massacre of 1850.* Berkeley: University of California Archaeological Research Facility, Department of Anthropology.

*[100]   1974. *They Were Only Diggers: A Collection of Articles from California Newspapers, 1851–1866, on Indian and White Relations.* Ballena Press Publications in Archaeology, Ethnology and History:1, ed. Robert F. Heizer. Ramona, Calif.: Ballena Press.

[101]   Heizer, Robert Fleming, ed. 1972. *George Gibbs' Journal of Redick McKee's Expedition Through Northwestern California in 1851.* Berkeley: University of California Archaeological Research Facility, Department of Anthropology.

*[102]   Heizer, Robert Fleming and Almquist, Alan J.

1971. *The Other Californians; Prejudice and Discrimination under Spain, Mexico and the United States to 1920.* Berkeley: University of California Press.

[103] Heizer, Robert Fleming and Elsasser, Albert B. 1970. *A Bibliography of California Archaeology.* Contributions of the University of California Archaeological Research Facility:6. Berkeley: University of California Archaeological Research Facility, Department of Anthropology. [An updated version is forthcoming.]

[104] Heizer, Robert Fleming and Hester, Thomas Roy. 1970. "Names and Locations of Some Ethnographic Patwin and Maidu Villages." Contributions of the University of California Archaeological Research Facility:9, *Papers on California Ethnography,* pp. 79–118. Berkeley: University of California Archaeological Research Facility, Department of Anthropology.

[105] Heizer, Robert Fleming and Mills, John E. 1952. *The Four Ages of Tsurai; A Documentary History of the Indian Village on Trinidad Bay.* Berkeley: University of California Press.

[106] Heizer, Robert Fleming and Nissen, Karen M. 1973. *The Human Sources of California Ethnography.* Berkeley: University of California Archaeological Research Facility, Department of Anthropology.

*[107]   Heizer, Robert Fleming and Treganza, Adan Eduardo. 1944. "Mines and Quarries of the Indians of California." *California Journal of Mines and Geology* 40:291–359. (Reprinted, Ramona Calif.: Ballena Press, 1972.)

[108]   Heizer, Robert Fleming and Whipple, Mary Anne, eds. 1971. *The California Indians; A Source Book*. 2nd ed., rev. and enl. Berkeley: University of California Press.

*[109]   Hoopes, Alban W. 1932. *Indian Affairs and Their Administration, With Special Reference to the Far West, 1849–1860*. Philadelphia: University of Pennsylvania Press.

[110]   Hudson, Millard F. 1907. "The Pauma Massacre." *Annual Publications of the Historical Society of Southern California* 7:13–21.

[111]   Hutchinson, Cecil Alan. 1969. *Frontier Settlement in Mexican California; The Hijar-Padres Colony and Its Origins, 1769–1835*. New Haven: Yale University Press.

[112]   Indian Board of Cooperation. *California Indian Herald*. 1923–31. Philadelphia.

Indian Rights Association, Inc.

[113]   *Annual Report*. 1882–   . Philadelphia. [Material germane to California Indians is to be found in the issues from 1888 to 1904, during which time

the publication was styled *Annual Report of the Executive Committee.*]

[114]   *Indian Truth.* 1924 –   . Philadelphia.

[115]   Inter-Tribal Council of California. *The Tribal Spokesman.* 1964 –   . Sacramento.

*[116]   Jackson, Helen Maria (Fiske) Hunt [published as H. H.]. 1881. *A Century of Dishonor; A Sketch of the United States Government's Dealings With Some of the Indian Tribes.* New York: Harper and Bros. and [a substantially similar version for British readers] London: Chatto and Windus. (Reprinted numerous times, the text is readily accessible through a Harper Torchbook version, ed. Andrew F. Rolle.)

[117]   Jackson, Helen Maria (Fiske) Hunt and Kinney, Abbot. 1883. *Report on the Condition and Needs of the Mission Indians of California, Made by Special Agents Helen Jackson and Abbot Kinney, to the Commissioner of Indian Affairs.* Washington, D.C.: Government Printing Office.

[118]   Jennings, Jesse David and Norbeck, Edward, eds. 1964. *Prehistoric Man in the New World.* Chicago: University of Chicago Press.

[119]   Johnson, Kenneth M. 1966. *K-344; or The Indians of California vs. the United States.* Los Angeles: Dawson's Book Shop.

*[120]   Kasch, C. 1947. "The Yokayo Rancheria." *California Historical Society Quarterly* 26:209 16.

Kelsey, C. E.

*[121]   1906. *Report of the Special Agent for California Indians to the Commissioner of Indian Affairs, March 21, 1906.* Carlisle, [Pa.]: Indian School Print.

[122]   1971. *Census of Non-Reservation California Indians, 1905–1906.* Berkeley: University of California Archaeological Research Facility, Department of Anthropology.

[123]   Kenny, Robert Walker. 1944. *History and Proposed Settlement, Claims of California Indians.* California, Attorney General's Office. Sacramento: California State Printing Office.

Kroeber, Alfred Louis.

*[124]   1905. "California Basketry and the Pomo." *American Anthropologist* 11:233–49.

[125]   1908. *A Mission Record of the California Indians.* University of California Publications in American Archaeology and Ethnology:8, pt. 1, pp. 1–27. Berkeley: University of California Press.

*[126]   1916. *California Place Names of Indian Origin.* University of California Publications in American Archaeology and Ethnology:12, pt. 2, pp. 31–69. Berkeley: University of California Press.

[127]   1922. *Basket Designs of the Mission Indians of Cali-*

fornia. Anthropological Papers of the American Museum of Natural History:20, pt. 2, pp. 149–83. New York: The Trustees. (Reprinted, with additional illustrations, Ramona, Calif.: Ballena Press, 1973.)

[128] 1925. *Handbook of the Indians of California.* Smithsonian Institution, Bureau of American Ethnology, Bulletin:78. Washington, D.C.: Government Printing Office.

[129] 1932. *The Patwin and Their Neighbors.* University of California Publications in American Archaeology and Ethnology:29, pt. 4, pp. 253–423. Berkeley: University of California Press.

[130] 1957. "California Indian Population About 1910." *University of California Publications in American Archaeology and Ethnology:* 47, pp. 218–25. Berkeley: University of California Press.

[131] 1962. *Two Papers on the Aboriginal Ethnography of California.* Reports of the University of California Archaeological Survey:56. Berkeley: University of California, Department of Anthropology.

[132] Kroeber, Alfred Louis and Gifford, Edward Winslow. 1949. *World Renewal: A Cult System of Native Northwest California.* Anthropological

Records:13, pp. 1–155. Berkeley: University of California Press.

[133] Kroeber, Alfred Louis and Heizer, Robert Fleming. 1970. "Continuity of Indian Population in California from 1770/1846 to 1955." Contributions of the University of California Archaeological Research Facility:9, *Papers on California Ethnography*, pp. 1–22. Berkeley: University of California Archaeological Research Facility, Department of Anthropology.

*[134] Kroeber, Theodora and Heizer, Robert Fleming. 1968. *Almost Ancestors: The First Californians*. San Francisco: The Sierra Club.

[135] Lathrop, Marion Lydia. 1932. "The Indian Campaigns of General M. G. Vallejo, Defender of the Northern Frontier of California." *Quarterly of the Society of California Pioneers* 9:161–205.

[136] Latta, Frank Forest. 1949. *Handbook of Yokuts Indians*. Bakersfield, Calif.: Kern County Museum.

[137] Lee, Dorothy Demetracopoulou. 1950. "Notes on the Concept of Self Among the Wintu Indians." *Journal of Abnormal Psychology* 45:538–43.

[138] Leonard, Zenas. 1904. *Adventures of Zenas Leonard, Fur Trader and Trapper, 1831–1836*, ed.

William Finley Wagner. Cleveland: The Burrows Bros. Co.

Loeb, Edwin Meyer.

[139] 1926. "The Creator Concept Among the Indians of North Central California." *American Anthropologist* 28:467–93.

[140] 1932. *The Western Kuksu Cult.* University of California Publications in American Archaeology and Ethnology:33, pt. 2, pp. 139–231. Berkeley: University of California Press.

[141] 1933. *The Eastern Kuksu Cult.* University of California Publications in American Archaeology and Ethnology:33, pt. 2, pp. 139–231. Berkeley: University of California Press.

[142] Loomis, Noel M. 1971. "The Garra Uprising of 1851." In *Brand Book II,* ed. Jim Darling, pp. 3–26. San Diego: The San Diego Corral of the Westerners.

[143] Lurie, Nancy Oestreich. 1957. "The Indian Claims Commission Act." *Annals of the American Academy of Political and Social Science* 311:56 –70.

[144] MacGregor, Gordon. 1939. "The Social and Economic Adjustment of the Indians of the Sacramento Jurisdiction of California." In *Proceedings of the Fifth Pacific Science Congress,* vol. 6, no. 4, pp. 53–58. Toronto: University of Toronto Press.

[145] Maloney, Alice Bay, ed. 1945. *Fur Brigade to the Bonaventura. John Work's California Expedition, 1832–1833 for the Hudson's Bay Company.* California Historical Society, Special Publication:19. San Francisco: California Historical Society.

[146] March, Ray. 1970. "On the 40th Day of the Indian Occupation of Alcatraz Island." *San Francisco Business* (Feb.), pp. 34–40.

[147] Meighan, Clement Woodward and Riddell, Francis A. 1972. *The Maru Cult of the Pomo Indians: A California Ghost Dance Survival.* Southwest Museum Papers:23. Los Angeles: Southwest Museum.

[148] Merriam, Clinton Hart. 1955. "The Expulsion of Sahte: A Stony Ford Pomo Ceremony." In *Studies of California Indians,* ed. Staff of the Department of Anthropology, University of California, pp. 29–37. Berkeley: University of California Press.

[149] Merrill, Ruth Earl. 1923. *Plants Used in Basketry by the California Indians.* University of California Publications in American Archaeology and Ethnology:20, pp. 213–42. Berkeley: University of California Press.

[150] Murray, Keith A. *The Modocs and Their War.* The

Civilization of the American Indian Series:52. Norman: University of Oklahoma Press.

[151] Murdock, George Peter. 1975. *Ethnographic Bibliography of North America.* 4th ed., rev. by Timothy J. O'Leary. 5 vols. New Haven: Human Relations Area Files Press.

[152] Northern California Indian Association. *Newsletter.* 1906–   . Mount Hermon, Calif.

[153] Oaks, Richard. 1972. "Alcatraz is Not an Island." *Ramparts* (Dec.), pp. 35–40; and 67.

[154] Oswalt, Robert L. 1958. "Russian Loan Words in Southwestern Pomo." *International Journal of American Linguistics* 24:245–47.

[155] Phillips, George Harwood. 1975. *Chiefs and Challengers: Indian Resistance and Cooperation in Southern California.* Berkeley and Los Angeles: University of California Press.

[156] Powell, John Wesley. 1891. "Indian Linguistic Families of America, North of Mexico." In *Seventh Annual Report* (1885/86), U. S. Bureau of American Ethnology, pp. 1–142. Washington, D.C.: Government Printing Office.

*[157] Powers, Stephen. 1877. *Tribes of California.* Department of the Interior, U.S. Geographical and Geological Survey of the Rocky Mountain Area, Contributions to North American

Ethnology:3. Washington, D.C.: Government Printing Office. (Reprinted, Berkely: University of California Press, 1976.)

[158] Quinn, Frank. 1956. *Indians of California: Past and Present.* San Francisco: American Friends Service Committee.

[159] Reichlen, Henri and Reichlen, Paulette. 1971. "Le manuscrit Boscana de la Bibliothèque Nationale de Paris." *Journal de la Société des Américanistes* 60:233–73.

[160] Reid, Hugo. 1968. *The Indians of Los Angeles County: Hugo Reid's Letters of 1852,* ed. Robert F. Heizer. Los Angeles: Southwest Museum.

[161] Riddle, Jeff C. 1914. *The Indian History of the Modoc War, and the Causes That Led to It.* San Francisco: Marnell and Co.

[162] Robinson, Alfred. 1846. *Life in California: During a Residence of Several Years in That Territory, Comprising a Description of the Country and the Missionary Establishments, with Incidents, Observations, etc., etc. . . . By an American. To Which is Annexed a Historical Account of the Origin, Customs, and Traditions, of the Indians of Alta-California. Tr. from the Original Spanish Manuscript.* New York: Wiley and Putnam. [Many subsequent editions do not contain the translation of the Boscana manuscript alluded to in the title.]

[163]   The Sequoyah League. *Bulletin.* 1904–11; Los
         Angeles. [The *Bulletin* grew out of articles ap-
         pearing in *Out West* under the editorship of
         Charles F. Lummis. For further information see
         Frances E. Watkins's 1944 article, "Charles F.
         Lummis and the Sequoyah League." *Historical
         Society of Southern California Quarterly*
         26:99–114.]

Shipley, William.

[164]   1962. "Spanish Elements in the Indigenous
         Languages of Central California." *Romance
         Philology* 16:1–21.

[165]   1974. "California." *Current Trends in Linguistics*
         10:1046–78.

[166]   Simoons, F. J. 1953. "Changes in Indian Life in
         the Clear Lake Area, Along the Northern
         Fringe of Mexican Influence in Early Cali-
         fornia." *Americana Indigena* 13:103–108.

*[167]   Spott, Robert and Kroeber, Alfred Louis. 1942.
         Yurok Narratives. University of California Pub-
         lications in American Archaeology and
         Ethnology:35, pt. 9, pp. 143–256. Berkeley:
         University of California Press.

[168]   Steward, Julian Haynes. 1936. *Myths of the Owens
         Valley Paiute.* University of California Publica-
         tions in American Archaeology and Ethnol-

ogy:34, pt. 5, pp. 355–439. Berkeley: University of California Press.

[169] Stewart, Omer Call. 1961. "Kroeber and the Indian Claims Commission Cases." *Kroeber Anthropological Society Papers* 25:181–90.

[170] Strong, William Duncan. 1929. *Aboriginal Society in Southern California.* University of California Publications in American Archaeology and Ethnology:26, pp. 1–358. Berkeley: University of California Press.

[171] Sutton, Imre. 1967. "Private Property in Land Among Reservation Indians in Southern California." *Yearbook of the Association of Pacific Coast Geographers* 29:69–89.

[172] Tac, Pablo. 1952. "Indian Life and Customs at Mission San Luis Rey: A Record of California Indian Life Written by Pablo Tac, an Indian Neophyte (Rome, 1835)," eds. and trans. Minna and Gordon Hewes. *Americas* 9:87–106.

[173] Toffelmeier, Gertrude and Luomela, Katherine. 1936. "Dreams and Dream Interpretation of the Diegueno Indians." *Psychoanalytic Quarterly* 5:195–225.

[174] United States Bureau of Indian Affairs. 1972. *California Rancheria Task Force Report.* Sac-

ramento: Bureau of Indian Affairs, California Office.

[175]   United States Congress, House. Committee on Indian Affairs. 1926. "Reservation Courts of Indian Offenses." 69th Congress, 1st session. Hearings Before the Committee on Indian Affairs on H. R. 7826. Washington, D.C.: Government Printing Office.

University of California.

[176]   Anthropological Records. 1937–   . Berkeley: University of California Press.

[177]   University of California Publications in American Archaeology and Ethnology. 1903–   . Berkeley: University of California Press. [Both serials contain studies issued under separate covers, paginated variously to reflect continuity within the larger corpus. For this reason, the Library of Congress catalogues such titles as individual monographs; that device has been followed here.]

Valory, Dale.

[178]   1966. "The Focus of Indian Shaker Healing." *Kroeber Anthropological Society Papers* 35:67–111.

[179]   1971. *Guide to Ethnological Documents (1–203) of the Department and Museum of Anthropology, University of California, Berkeley, now in the University*

Archives. Berkeley: University of California Archaelogical Research Facility, Department of Anthropology.

[180] Wagner, Henry Raup. 1929. *Spanish Voyages to the Northwest Coast of America in the Sixteenth Century*. California Historical Society, Special Publication:4. San Francisco: California Historical Society.

*[181] Washburn, Wilcomb E. 1971. *Red Man's Land/White Man's Law*. New York: Charles Scribner's Sons.

[182] Washburn, Wilcomb E., comp. 1973. *The American Indian and the United States: A Documentary History*. 4 vols. New York: Charles Scribner's Sons.

Waterman, Thomas Talbot.

*[183] 1909. "Analysis of the Mission Indian Creation Story." *American Anthropologist* 11:41–55.

[184] 1920. *Yurok Geography*. University of California Publications in American Archaeology and Ethnology:16, pt. 5, pp. 177–314. Berkeley: University of California Press.

[185] Watkins, Frances Emma. 1944. "Charles F. Lummis and the Sequoyah League." See [163].

[186] Webb, Ernest B. 1965. *American Indians of California*. San Francisco: California State Depart-

ment of Industrial Relations, Division of Fair Employment Practices.

*[187]   Weber, Francis J. 1968. "The California Missions and Their Visitors." *Americas* 24:319–36.

[188]   Wetmore, Charles Augustus. 1875. *Report of Chas. A. Wetmore, Special U.S. Commissioner of Mission Indians of Southern California.* Washington, D.C.: Government Printing Office.

White, Raymond C.

[189]   1957. "The Luiseño Theory of 'Knowledge'." *American Anthropologist* 59:1–19.

[190]   1963. *Luiseño Social Organization.* University of California Publications in American Archaeology and Ethnology:48, pt. 2, pp. 91–194. Berkeley: University of California Press.

[191]   Willey, Gordon Randolph. 1966. *An Introduction to American Archaeology.* 2 vols. Englewood Cliffs, N.J.: Prentice-Hall. [Volume 1, *North and Middle America,* is apposite to California studies.]

*[192]   Willoughby, Nona C. 1963. *Division of Labor Among the Indians of California.* Reports of the University of California Archaeological Survey:60, pp. 1–80. Berkeley: University of California, Department of Anthropology.

[193]   Wilson, Birbeck. 1968. *Ukiah Valley Pomo Religious Life, Supernatural Doctoring, and Beliefs: Ob-*

servations of 1939–1941. Reports of the University of California Archaeological Survey:72. Berkeley: University of California, Department of Anthropology.

ARTIFACT REPOSITORIES
  Banning, Calif. Malki Museum.
  Berkeley. University of California, Lowie Museum of Anthropology.
  Chicago. Field Museum of Natural History.
  Los Angeles. Southwest Museum.
  Milwaukee. Milwaukee Public Museum.
  New York. American Museum of Natural History.
  San Diego. Museum of Man.
  Washington. United States National Museum of Natural History.

MANUSCRIPT REPOSITORIES
  Berkeley. University of California.
    Bancroft Library.
    Department of Anthropology, C. Hart Merriam Collection.
    University Archives.
  Sacramento. California State Library.
  San Francisco. California Historical Society.
  San Marino. Huntington Library.

PICTORIAL REPOSITORIES

Berkeley. University of California.

Department of Anthropology, C. Hart Merriam Collection.

Lowie Museum of Anthropology

Bancroft Library

Los Angeles. Southwest Museum.

Sacramento. California State Library.

San Francisco. California Historical Society.

Washington. Smithsonian Institution, National Anthropological Archives.

The Newberry Library
Center for the History of the American Indian

Director: Francis Jennings

Established in 1972 by the Newberry Library, in conjunction with the Committee on Institutional Cooperation of eleven midwestern universities, the Center makes the resources of one of America's foremost research libraries in the Humanities available to those interested in improving the quality and effectiveness of teaching American Indian history. The Newberry's collections include some 100,000 volumes on the history of the American Indian and offer specialized resources for studying historical aspects of Indian–White relations and Indian linguistics. The Center also assists Native Americans engaged in writing tribal histories and developing educational materials.

ADVISORY COMMITTEE

Chairman: D'Arcy McNickle